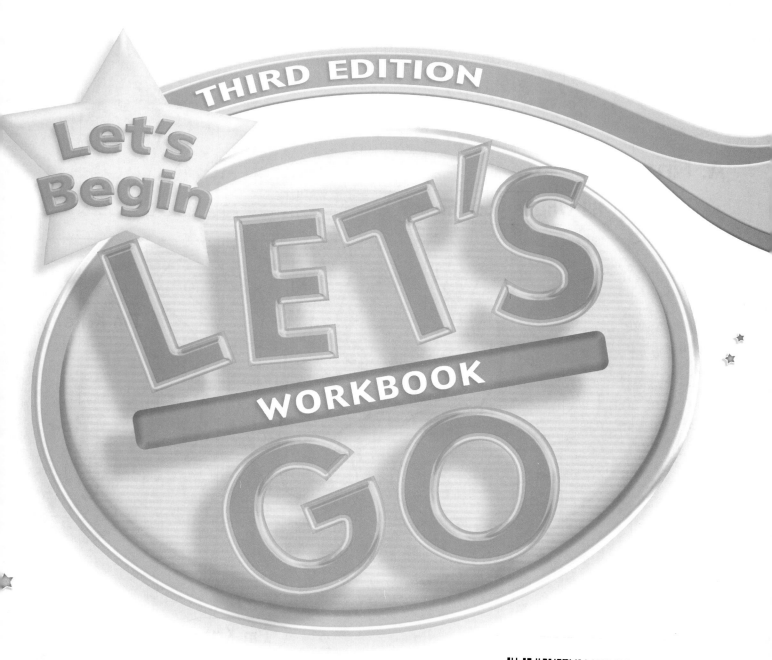

THIRD EDITION

Let's Begin

LET'S

WORKBOOK

GO

T0346865

Kathryn O'Dell

Ritsuko Nakata

Karen Frazier

Barbara Hoskins

OXFORD

UNIVERSITY PRESS

 Let's Start

A. Find Kate.

B. Circle.

1.

2.

3.

4.

C. Match.

1.

What's your name?

I'm Scott.

2.

What's your name?

I'm Kate.

3.

What's your name?

I'm Jenny.

D. ✓ or X.

1.

Stand up.

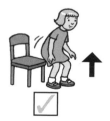

☑

☒

☐

2.

Sit down.

☐

☐

☐

Let's Learn

A. Match.

1. 2. 3. 4.

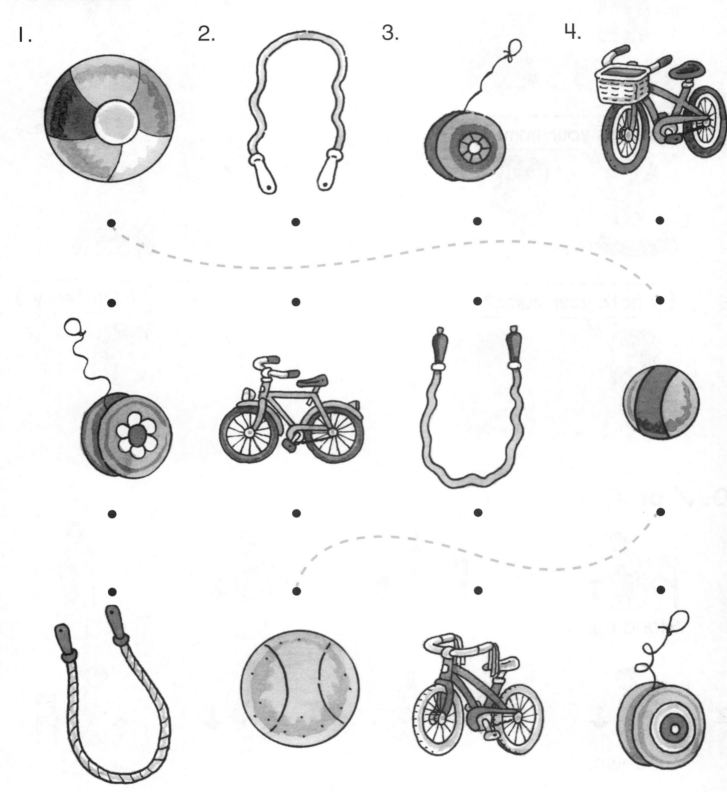

B. Find and circle.

It's a ball.

It's a jump rope.

It's a yo-yo.

It's a bicycle.

Let's Learn More

A. Trace and color.

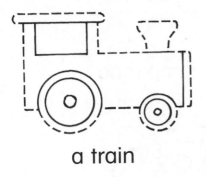

a train

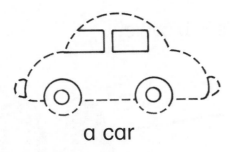

a car

a doll

a teddy bear

B. Match.

1. It's a train.

2. It's a car.

3. It's a doll.

4. It's a teddy bear.

C. Match and say.

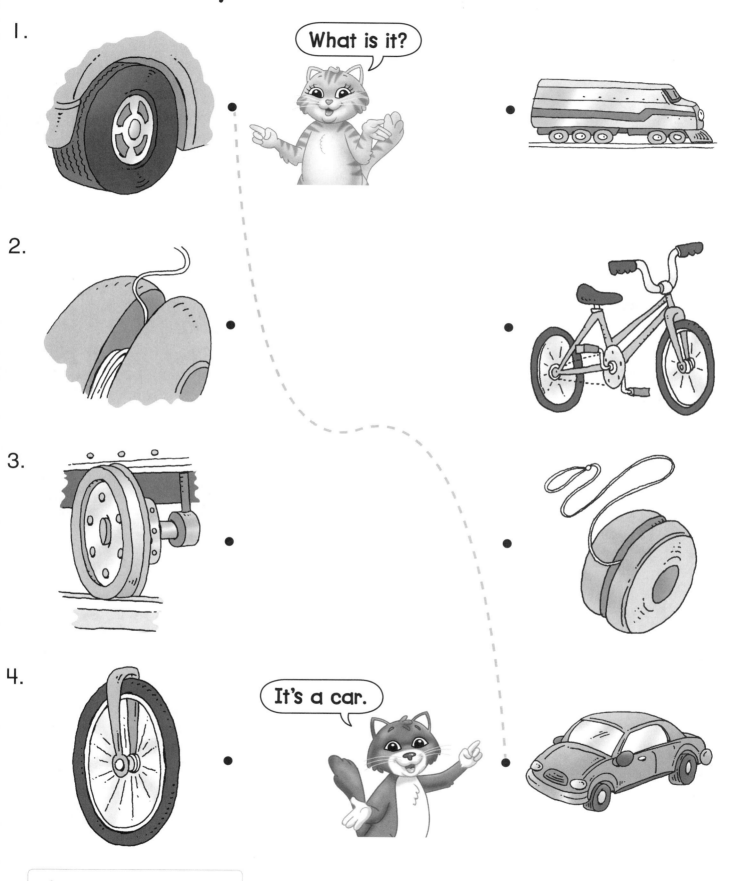

The Alphabet

A. Connect.

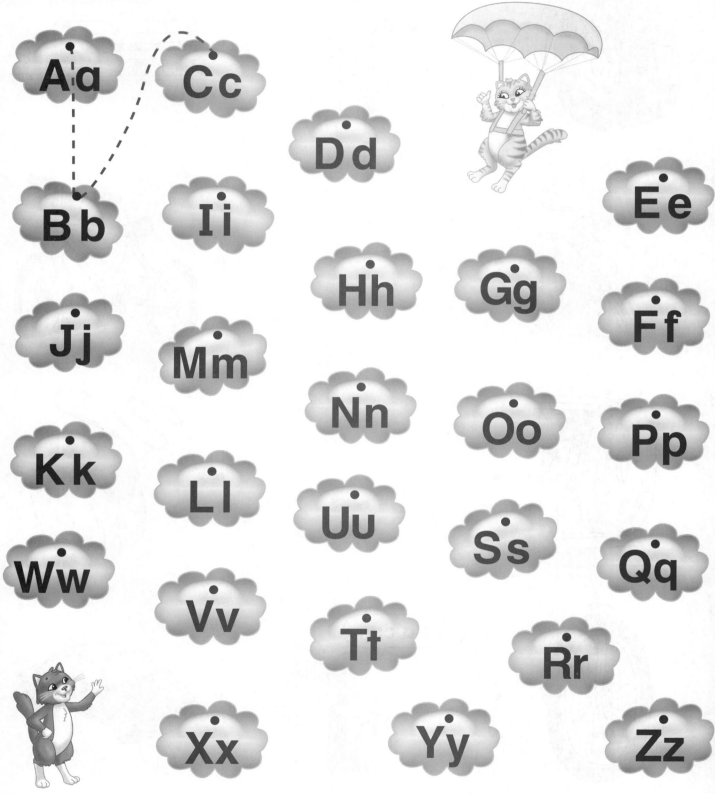

Aa Cc

Dd

Bb Ii Ee

Hh Gg Ff

Jj Mm

Nn Oo Pp

Kk Ll Uu Ss Qq

Ww Vv Tt Rr

Xx Yy Zz

Let's Build

A. Match.

What's your name?

What is it?

1.

I'm Ann.

It's a doll.

2.

I'm Matt.

It's a yo-yo.

3.

I'm Beth.

It's a train.

4.

I'm Pete.

It's a jump rope.

Unit 2 Colors

Let's Start

A. Find.

B. Match and say.

C. ✓ or X.

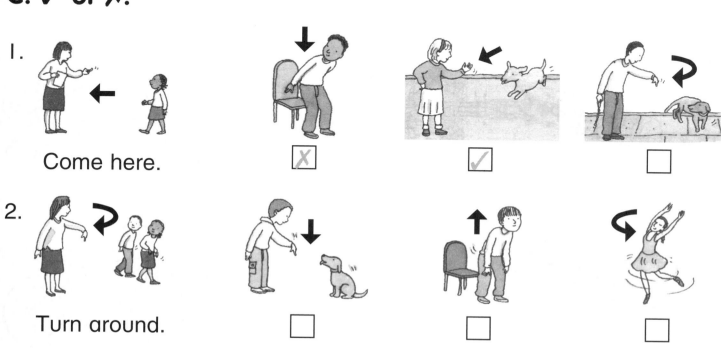

1. Come here.   ☒   ☑   ☐

2. Turn around.   ☐   ☐   ☐

Let's Learn

A. Match and color.

1.

red

2.

blue

3.

yellow

4.

green

5.

brown

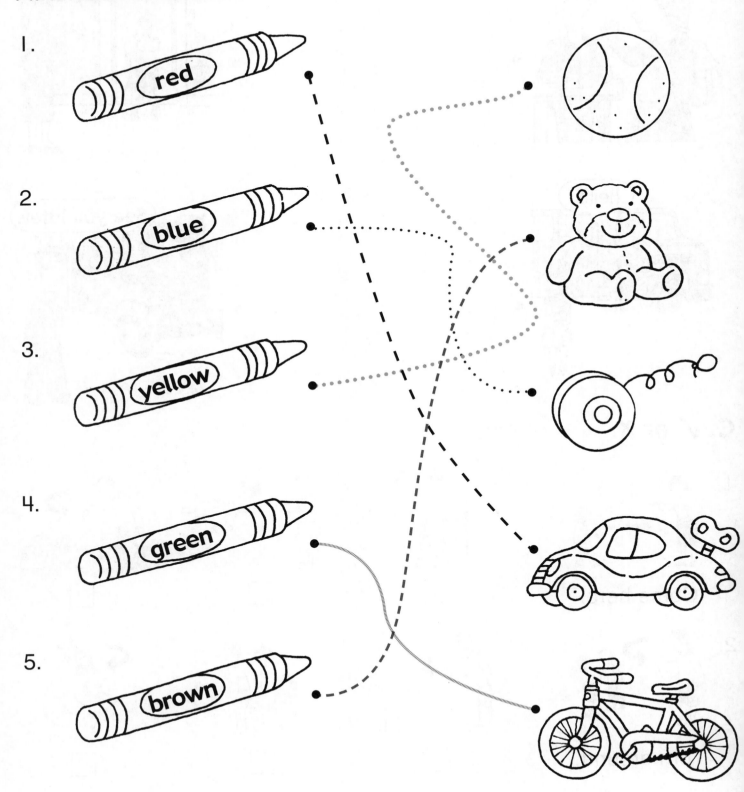

B. Trace and color.

1.

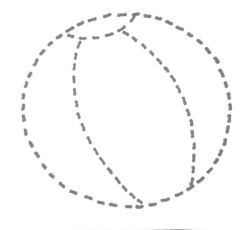

It's red.

2.

It's blue.

3.

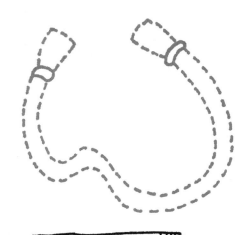

It's green.

4.

It's yellow.

5.

It's brown.

Let's Learn More _____

A. Color.

1.

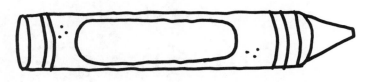

It's white.

2.

It's orange.

3.

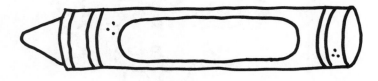

It's purple.

4.

It's pink.

5.

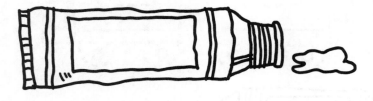

It's black.

B. Find and color.

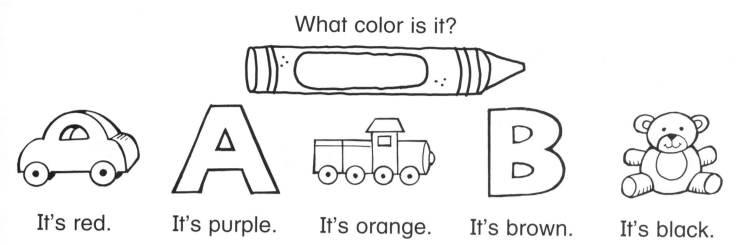

What color is it?

It's red.   It's purple.   It's orange.   It's brown.   It's black.

TOYS

The Alphabet _____

A. Circle and say.

1. **A**

c

(a)

A

D

B

2. **B**

B

d

a

C

b

3. **C**

A

c

d

C

c

4. **D**

a

c

D

B

d

B. Trace and match.

1. •

2. •

3. •

4. •

 **Let's Build** _____

A. Match and color.

What is it?

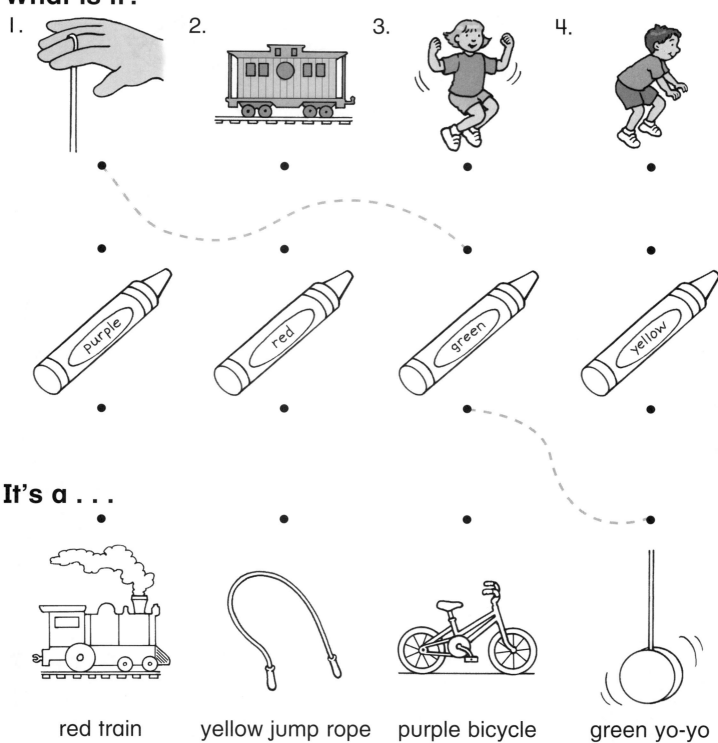

1.

2.

3.

4.

purple

red

green

yellow

It's a . . .

red train   yellow jump rope   purple bicycle   green yo-yo

Units 1-2 Let's Review

A. Match and color.

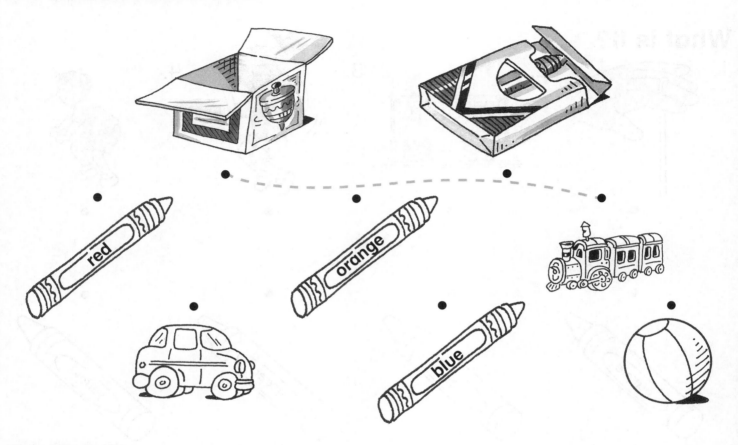

B. Match.

1.

Walk.

2.

Stand up.

3.

Sit down.

4.

Turn around.

School Supplies

A. Match and trace.

1.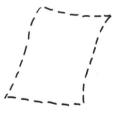

paper

2.

scissors

3.

glue

4.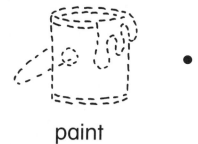

paint

5.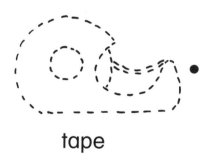

tape

I have scissors.

I have paint.

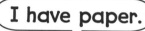

I have paper.

I have tape.

I have glue.

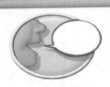 Let's Start

A. Match.

1.

How are you today?

I'm fine.

2.

How are you today?

I'm fine, thanks.

3.

How are you today?

I'm fine, thank you.

B. ✓ or X.

1.
 Walk.
 ☒
 ✓
 ☐

2.
 Run.
 ☐
 ☐
 ☐

C. Match.

Stand up. Walk. Turn around. Run. Sit down.

 •  •  •  •  •

 •  •  •

• 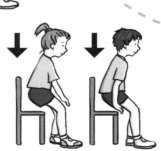 •

 # Let's Learn

A. Trace.

1.

a circle

2.

a square

3.

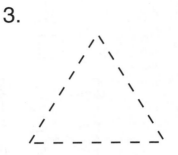

a triangle

4.

a heart

B. Complete the pattern.

1.

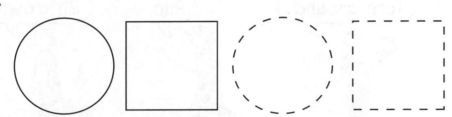

2.

3.

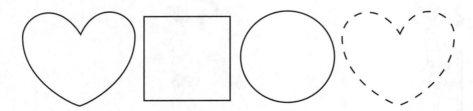

C. Trace. Then draw.

1.

Draw a circle.

2.

Draw a triangle.

3.

Draw a square.

4.

Draw a heart.

Let's Learn More

A. Match and circle.

1.

a star

2.
a rectangle

3.

a diamond

4.
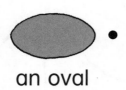
an oval

B. Trace.

a star

a rectangle

a diamond

an oval

C. Complete the pattern.

Is it a star?

Yes, it is.

1. Is it an oval?

No, it isn't. It's a heart.

2. Is it a triangle?

Yes, it is.

The Alphabet

A. Circle and say.

1. **EFGH**

   a b c d

   (E F G H)

   B C D E

   c d e f

   E F G H

2. **efgh**

   d e f g

   e f g h

   D E F G

   e f g h

   C D E F

B. Trace and circle.

1.

2.

3.

4.

Let's Build

A. Color and say.

1.

It's a blue square!

a blue square

2.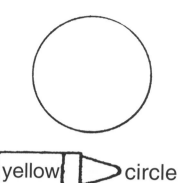

a yellow circle

3.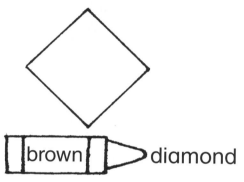

a brown diamond

4.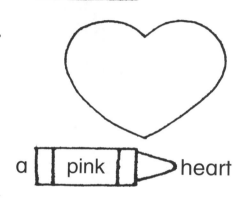

a pink heart

B. ✓ or ✗.

1.

Is it a black triangle?

Yes, it is.

 ✗

 ✓

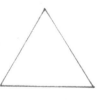 ☐

2.

Is it a red oval?

No, it isn't. It's a white star.

 ☐

 ☐

 ☐

✓

Let's Start

A. Match or X.

1.

2.

3.

4.

5.

B. Circle.

1. Go.

2. Stop.

3. Come here.

4. Turn around.

5. Sit down.

Let's Learn

A. Trace.

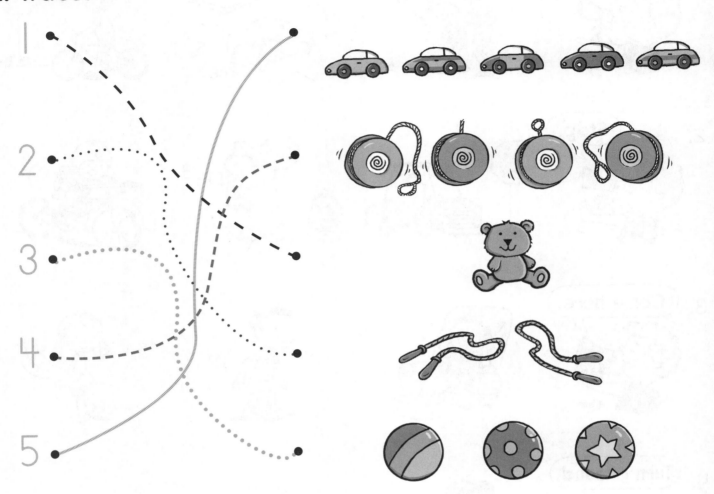

B. Color.

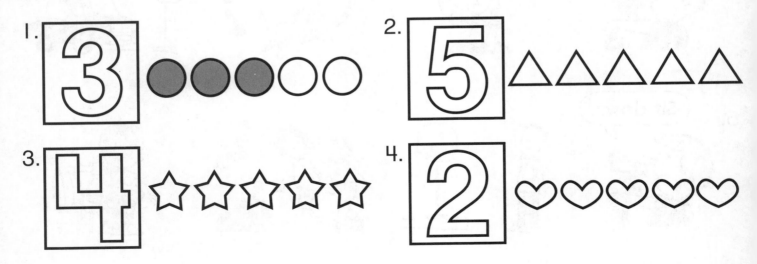

1. 3
2. 5
3. 4
4. 2

C. Draw and say.

Let's count.

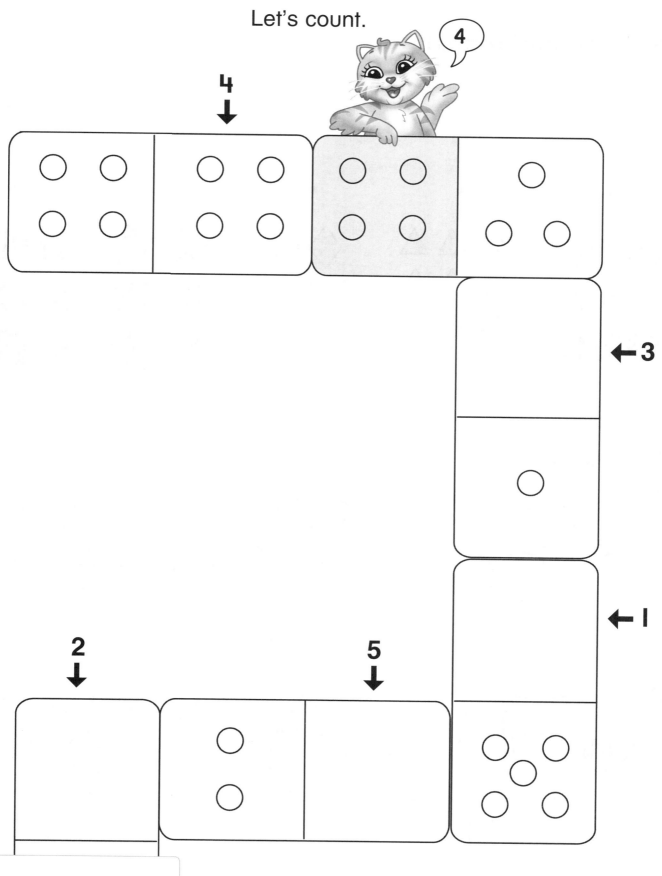

Let's Learn More

A. Trace and match.

6   7   8   9   10

B. ✓ or ✗.

1.

7   ✗   ✓   ☐

2.

10 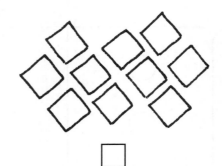 ☐    ☐   ☐

C. How many?

1.

   _6_

2.

   ___

3.

   ___

4.

   ___

5.

   ___

6.

   ___

The Alphabet

A. Draw.

I i = △   J j = ○   K k = □   L l = ♡

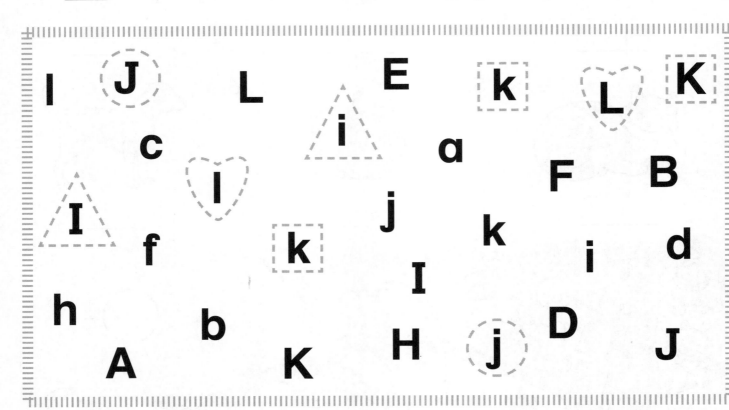

I   J   L   E   k   L   K

c   i   a

l   F   B

I   j   k   d

f   k   i

I

h   b   D   J

A   K   H   j

B. Trace and match.

1.

2.

3.

4.

 **Let's Build**

A. Finish the numbers.

1.

Is it a 1?

Yes, it is.

2.

Is it a 4?

No, it isn't. It's a 10.

3.

Is it a 2?

No, it isn't. It's a 7.

4.

Is it a 9?

Yes, it is.

Units 3-4 Let's Review

A. Find and circle.

1.
2.
3.
4.

Classroom Commands

A. Circle.

1. Take out your pencil.

2. Close your book.

3. Open your book.

4. Put away your pencil.

Let's Start

A. Match.

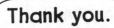

1.

2.

3.

B. Match.

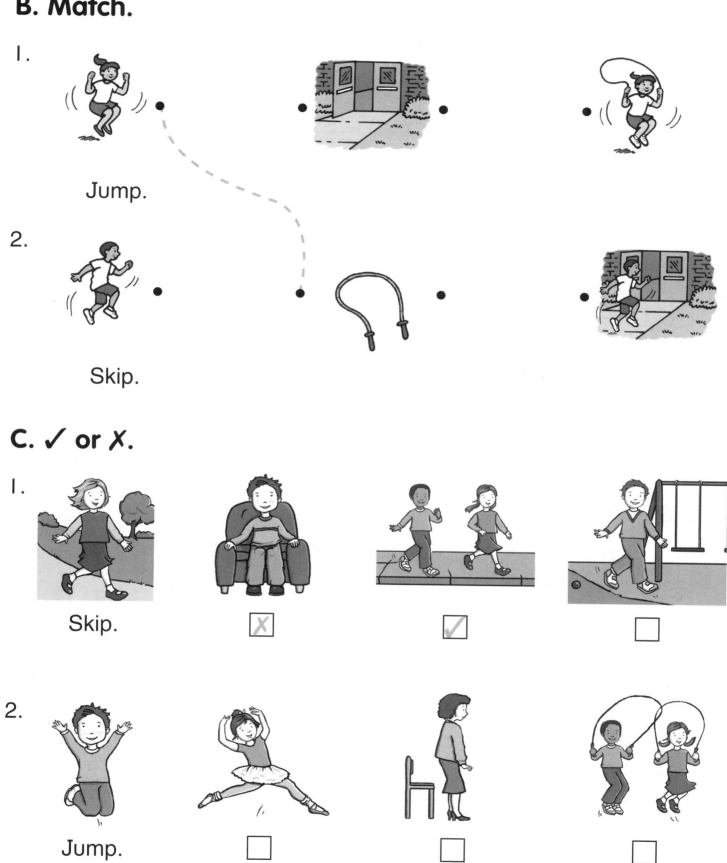

1.

Jump.

2.

Skip.

C. ✓ or ✗.

1.

Skip.

✗   ✓   ☐

2.

Jump.

☐   ☐   ☐

✓

 **Let's Learn**

A. Number.

1.

bird

2.

cat

3.

dog

4.

birds

5.

cats

6.

dogs

B. How many? Write and say.

Let's count the cats.

1 cat, 2 cats, 3 cats!

1. __3__ cats

2. ____ bird

3. ____ dogs

4. ____ dog

5. ____ cat

6. ____ birds

Let's Learn More

A. Find.

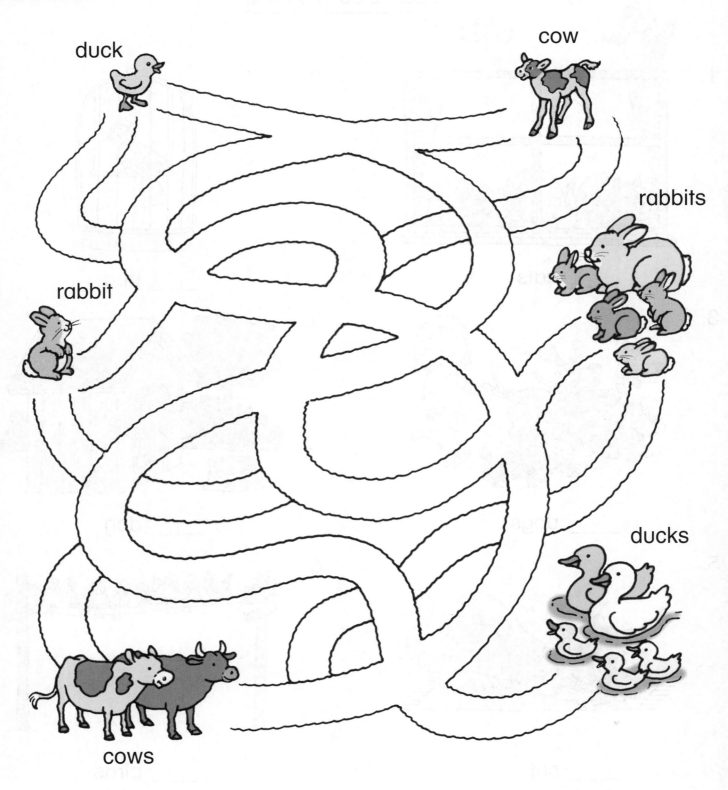

duck

cow

rabbits

rabbit

ducks

cows

B. Count and write.

1. How many cows? $\underline{4}$ cows.

2. How many ducks?   _____ ducks.

3. How many dogs?   _____ dog.

4. How many birds?   _____ birds.

5. How many rabbits?   _____ rabbits.

✓

The Alphabet _____

A. Find and circle.

```
A   M   N   O   P   A   m   n   o   p
C   a   L   b   o   p   K   j   i   M
m   N   O   D   M   N   O   P   h   n
n   m   n   o   p   g   m   n   o   p
M   N   O   P   f   E   n   F   l   B
N   H   P   m   n   o   p   G   P   k
p   c   I   d   e   M   N   O   P   J
```

B. Trace and match.

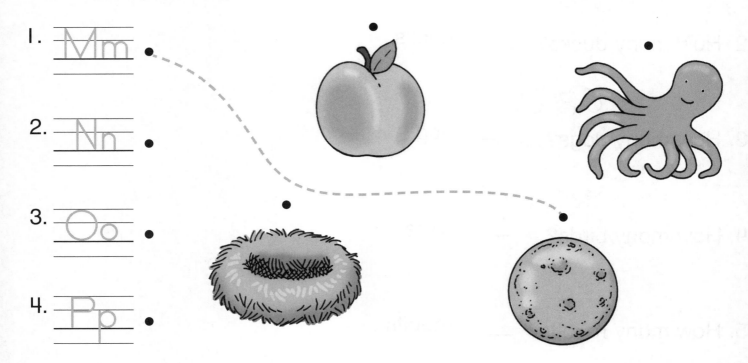

1. Mm •
2. Nn •
3. Oo •
4. Pp •

Let's Build

A. Match, count, and say.

1.       How many dolls?

2.

3.

4.    1 doll, 2 dolls, 3 dolls!

Unit 6 Food

A. Draw.

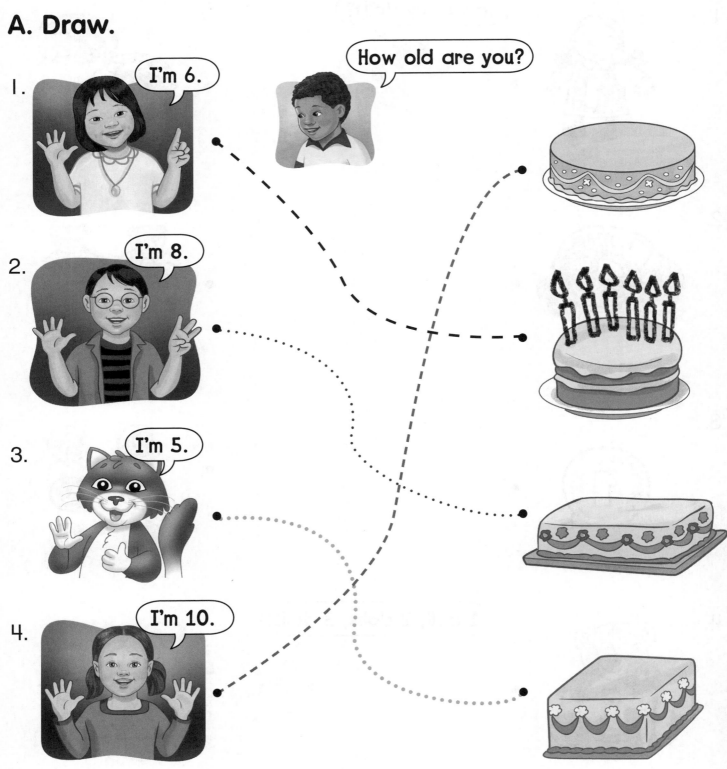

B. Draw and color.

C. ✓ or X.

1. Make a line.　　　X　　　✓　　　☐

2. Make a circle.　　　☐　　　☐　　　☐

Let's Learn

A. Match.

1. ice cream

2. pizza

3. cake

4. chicken

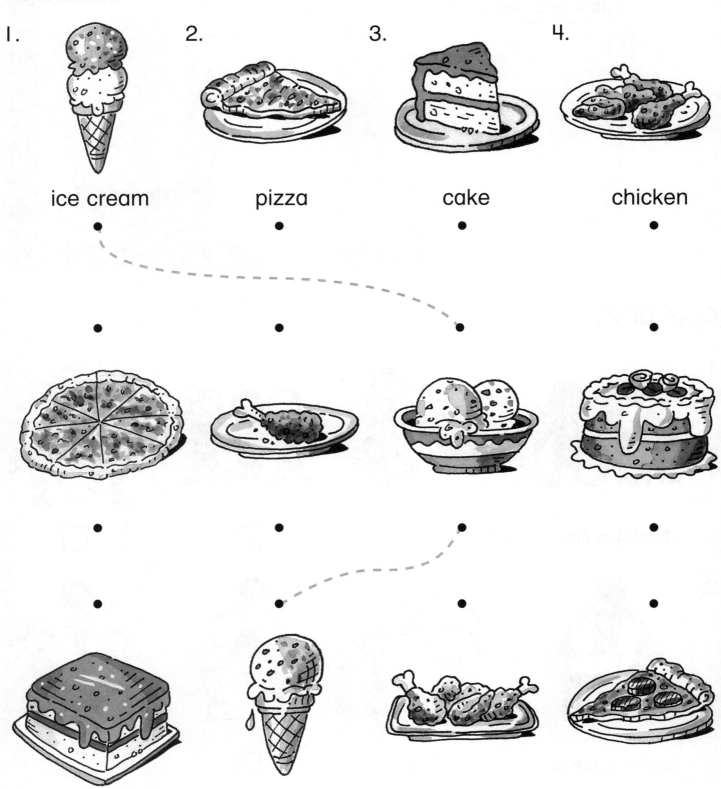

B. Number.

1.
I like pizza.

2.
I like chicken.

3.
I like cake.

4.
I like ice cream.

Let's Learn More

A. Circle.

1.

milk

2.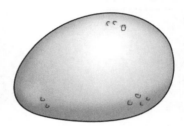

rice

3.

bread

4.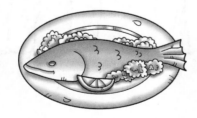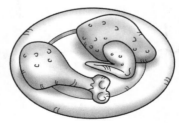

fish

B. Find.

The Alphabet

A. ✓ or X.

1. QRST

FGHI	QRST	OPQR
☒	☑	☐

2. qrst

defg	pqrs	qrst
☐	☐	☐

3. QrsT

QRST	qRsT	QrsT
☐	☐	☐

B. Trace and match.

1. Q •

2. R •

3. S •

4. T •

sun

tiger

rabbit

queen

 # Let's Build

A. Do you like _____ ? Circle and say.

1. Do you like milk?

Yes, I do.

No, I don't.

2. Do you like rice?

3. Do you like rabbits?

4. Do you like birds?

5. Do you like dolls?

6. Do you like cars?

A. Match.

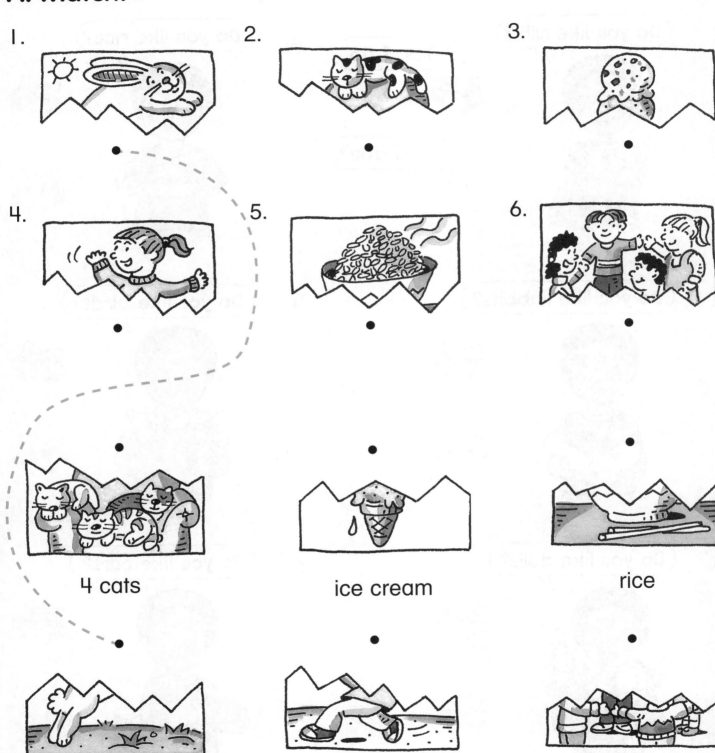

1.

2.

3.

4.

5.

6.

4 cats

ice cream

rice

1 rabbit

Skip.

Make a circle.

The Weather

A. Match and trace.

1.
sunny

2.
cloudy

3.
windy

4.
rainy

5.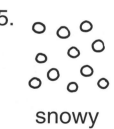
snowy

It's rainy.

It's cloudy.

It's sunny.

It's windy.

It's snowy.

Let's Start

A. Match.

1.

2.

3.

B. Match.

Clap your hands.   Stamp your feet.

1.
2.
3.
4.
5.

C. Number.

1.   2.   3.   4.   5.

Sit down.   Run.   Walk.

Jump.   Skip.

A. Circle.

1.

head

2.

shoulders

3.

knees

4.

toes

B. Match.

1.

I can touch my knees.

2.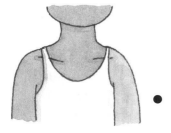

I can touch my shoulders.

3.

I can touch my head.

4.

I can touch my toes.

Let's Learn More

A. Match.

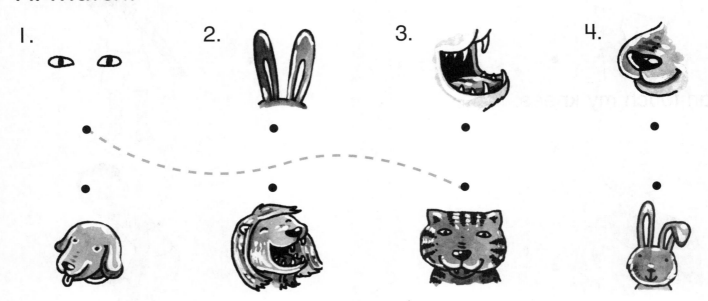

1.   2.   3.   4.

B. Draw.

eyes

ears

nose

mouth

C. Number.

What can you do?

1.

2.

3.

4.

5.

6.

I can touch my ears.

I can touch my eyes.

I can touch my mouth.

I can touch my knees.

1

I can touch my nose.

I can touch my toes.

✓

The Alphabet

A. Circle and say.

1. U

2. V

3. W

B. Trace and match.

1. U •

2. V •      • U

3. W •      • V

   • W

Let's Build

A. Number.

train

black triangle

white yo-yo

doll

white star

jump rope

teddy bear

black umbrella

Let's Start

A. Find.

B. Write 1 or 2.

1.  2

2.  ☐

3.  ☐

4.  ☐

C. ✓ or X.

1. Go to the board.

  X  ✓  ☐

2. Point to the board.

  ☐  ☐  ☐

✓

 # Let's Learn

A. Match.

1.

2.

3.

4.

fly a kite

sing a song

bounce a ball

ride a bicycle

B. Match and say.

I can ...

I can't ...

I can ride a bicycle.

I can't ride a bicycle.

1.

2.

3.

4.

✓

Let's Learn More

A. Find and circle.

wink

smile

swim

dance

B. Circle.

1.

2.

3.

4.

The Alphabet

A. Draw.

X x = ◇　　　Y y = ◯　　　Z z = ▭

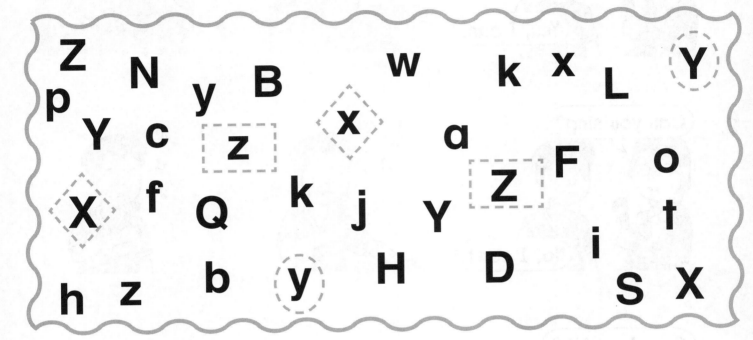

B. Trace and circle.

1. 　　fox

2. 　　yarn

3. 　　　zebra

Let's Build

A. Can you _____? Circle and say.

1. Can you wink?

 Yes, I can.

 No, I can't.

2. Can you jump?

3. Can you swim?

4. Can you fly a kite?

5. Can you touch your toes?

6. Can you skip?

Units 7-8 Let's Review

A. Find and number.

1 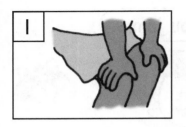	2	3 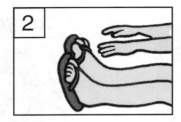	4 

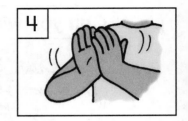

5 	6 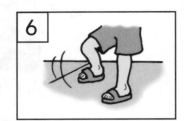	7 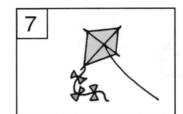	8 

Days of the Week

A. Match.

Sunday	Monday	Tuesday	Wednesday	Thursday	Friday	Saturday
1	2	3	4	5	6	7

1.
Monday
2

2.
Saturday
7

7.
Tuesday
3

3.
Sunday
1

6.
Thursday
5

4.
Wednesday
4

5.
Friday
6

Alphabet Practice _____

A. Color and trace.

B. Color and trace.

heart →

gorilla →

egg ↓

fish →

E e   F f   G g   H h

C. Color and trace.

igloo →

kangaroo ←

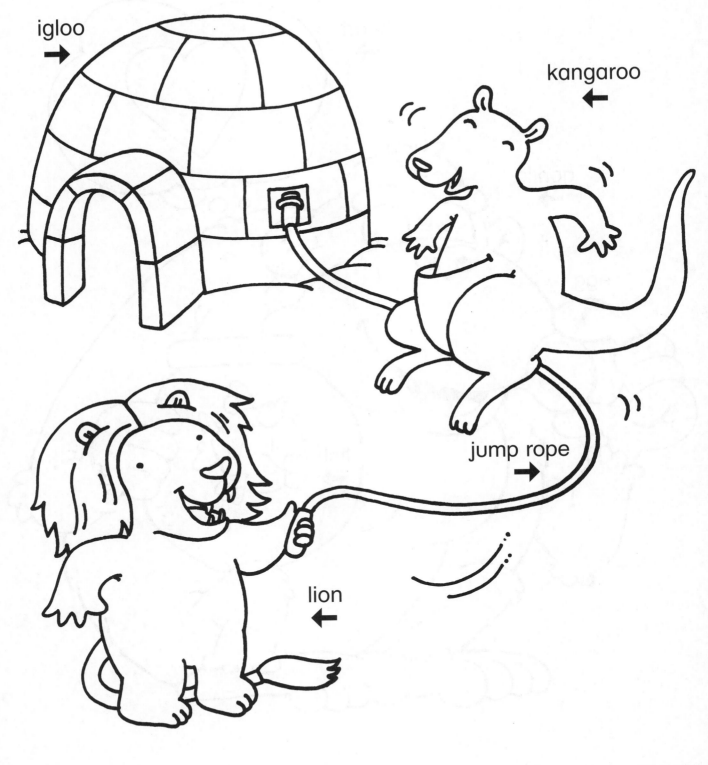

jump rope →

lion ←

D. Color and trace.

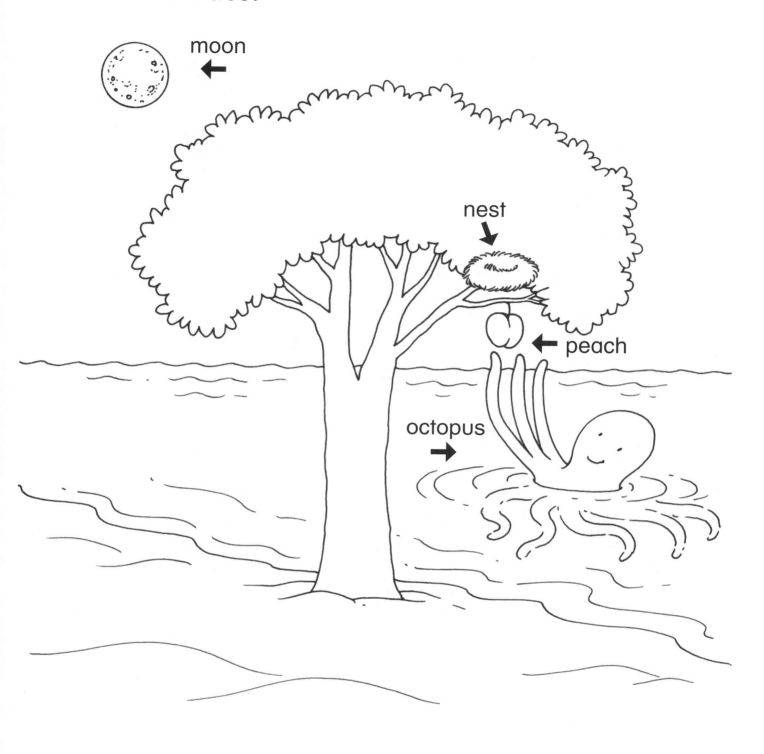

moon

nest

peach

octopus

M m   N n   O o   P p

E. Color and trace.

queen

sun

rabbit

tiger

Q q   R r   S s   T t

F. Color and trace.

umbrella

violin

watch

U U U u

V V V v

W W W w

G. Color and trace.

yarn ←

zebra →

fox ←

X X x   Y Y y   Z Z z